COOL
MAKERSPACE
GADGETS & GIZMOS

CODE IT!
PROGRAMMING AND KEYBOARDS
YOU CAN CREATE YOURSELF

Jessie Alkire

Checkerboard
Library

An Imprint of Abdo Publishing
abdopublishing.com

abdopublishing.com

Published by Abdo Publishing, a division of ABDO, PO Box 398166, Minneapolis, Minnesota 55439. Copyright © 2018 by Abdo Consulting Group, Inc. International copyrights reserved in all countries. No part of this book may be reproduced in any form without written permission from the publisher. Checkerboard Library™ is a trademark and logo of Abdo Publishing.

Printed in the United States of America, North Mankato, Minnesota
102017
012018

THIS BOOK CONTAINS
RECYCLED MATERIALS

Design: Sarah DeYoung, Mighty Media, Inc.
Production: Mighty Media, Inc.
Editor: Liz Salzmann
Cover Photographs: Mighty Media, Inc.; Richard Thomas © 123RF.com; Shutterstock
Interior Photographs: iStockphoto; Jay Silver/Flickr; Mighty Media, Inc.; Richard Thomas © 123RF.com; Shutterstock

The following manufacturers/names appearing in this book are trademarks: Makey Makey®, Play-Doh®, Scotch®, Sharpie®

Publisher's Cataloging-in-Publication Data
Names: Alkire, Jessie, author.
Title: Code it! programming and keyboards you can create yourself / by Jessie Alkire.
Other titles: Programming and keyboards you can create yourself
Description: Minneapolis, Minnesota : Abdo Publishing, 2018. |
    Series: Cool makerspace gadgets & gizmos | Includes online resources and index.
Identifiers: LCCN 2017944030 | ISBN 9781532112508 (lib.bdg.) |
    ISBN 9781614799924 (ebook)
Subjects: LCSH: Computer programming--Juvenile literature. |
    Creative ability in science--Juvenile literature. | Handicraft--Juvenile literature. | Makerspaces--Juvenile literature.
Classification: DDC 005.1--dc23
LC record available at https://lccn.loc.gov/2017944030

TO ADULT HELPERS

This is your chance to assist a young maker as they develop new skills, gain confidence, and make cool things! These activities are designed to help children create projects in makerspaces. Children may need more assistance for some activities than others. Be there to offer guidance when they need it. Encourage them to do as much as they can on their own. Be a cheerleader for their creativity.

Before getting started, remember to lay down ground rules for using tools and supplies and for cleaning up. There should always be adult supervision when using a hot or sharp tool.

CONTENTS

What's a MAKERSPACE?

Imagine a room buzzing with activity. All around you, programmers and crafters are working on super-cool projects. Welcome to a makerspace!

Makerspaces are areas where people come together to create. They are the perfect places to make amazing projects using keyboards and coding! Makerspaces are full of all kinds of supplies and tools. But a maker's most important tool is his or her imagination. Makers think of brand-new coding and keyboard projects. They also find ways to tweak existing projects. Makers are great problem solvers. Are you ready to become a maker?

BEFORE YOU GET STARTED

GET PERMISSION

Ask an adult for **permission** to use the makerspace and materials before starting any project.

BE RESPECTFUL

Share tools and supplies with other makers. When you're done with a tool, put it back so others can use it.

MAKE A PLAN

Read through the instructions and gather all your supplies ahead of time. Keep supplies organized as you create!

ASK FOR HELP

Working with computers and keyboards can be difficult. Ask an adult for help when you need it.

WHAT IS CODING?

Coding is creating instructions that tell a computer what to do. This process is also called programming. Computers control phones, video games, cars, and more. Coding is what makes these **technologies** work! The computers in these devices receive instructions in special coded languages. One is called binary. It uses only 1s and 0s. Other coding languages include Java, JavaScript, C, Perl, and more. Learning to code is like learning a new language! There are many **software** programs and building materials you can use to create computer codes.

SCRATCH

Scratch is an **online** coding program. With Scratch, you can code your own music, games, characters, and more. The characters in Scratch are called Sprites. You can tell Sprites what to do by choosing different Scripts. Scripts are Scratch's coding language. Many of the projects in this book use Scratch. The program can be found online at scratch.mit.edu.

MAKEY MAKEY

Makey Makey is a tool you can use to make your own keyboards and more! You can connect the Makey Makey board to a computer with a USB cable. Then, use wires to connect objects to the Makey Makey board. When you touch a connected object, Makey Makey sends a keyboard message to the computer. Your object has become a keyboard! Many projects in this book use Makey Makey.

SUPPLIES

Here are some of the materials and tools used for the projects in this book. If your makerspace doesn't have what you need, don't worry! Find different supplies to substitute for the missing materials. Or modify the project to fit the supplies you have. Be creative!

alligator
clips

aluminum
tape

beads

bracelet
memory wire

computer

double-sided
tape

Makey Makey
board

marker

needle-nose
pliers

pencil

Play-Doh

poster board

ruler

scissors

USB cable

wire

wire cutter

CODE IT!
TECHNIQUES

SCRATCH TUTORIALS

Scratch has many tutorials for beginning coders on their website. These tutorials show how Scratch works. They also describe the functions of each Script in the program. Read these descriptions to learn the basics. Then practice Scratch tutorials to get comfortable using the program before making your projects!

MAKE IT CONDUCTIVE!

Makey Makey needs to be connected to objects that are conductive. Objects that are conductive are able to conduct, or transport, electricity. Conductive materials that work well with Makey Makey include Play-Doh, fruit, and aluminum foil or aluminum tape. Aluminum tape can also be stuck to any object to make it conductive.

CODING BRACELET

Build a bracelet that spells your name in binary code!

WHAT YOU NEED

marker

paper

computer

beads in three different colors

bracelet memory wire

wire cutter • needle-nose pliers

1. Write your name vertically on paper. Then find an ASCII binary code chart **online**. Use it as a guide to write each letter's binary code beside it.

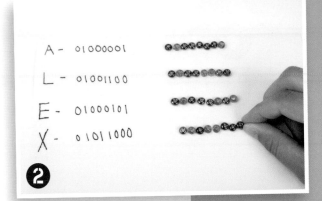

2. Pick one color bead to represent 0s and another color to represent 1s. Arrange the beads next to each letter to match the letter's code. The third color of bead will be used for spacing.

3. Cut a long length of bracelet memory wire. Use a pliers to make a closed loop at one end of the wire.

4. String three of the spacing beads onto the wire.

5. String the beads from each letter onto the wire. Add a spacing bead between each letter.

6. After the last letter, add spacing beads until the bracelet is the length you want it to be.

7. Cut the wire ½ inch (1.25 cm) after the last bead. Bend the end into a loop. Your new bracelet is ready to wear!

11

CODE A CHARACTER

Practice basic Scratch commands that bring a character to life!

WHAT YOU NEED

computer with Internet

Choose a Character and Backdrop

1. Go to scratch.mit.edu.

2. Click "Try It Out" on the Scratch home page. The program will display a cat as your character, or Sprite. To choose a different character, click the first icon next to "New sprite." This opens the Sprite Library.

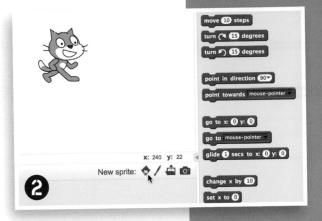

3. Click on the Sprite you want and then click "OK." The new Sprite will appear on the screen and in your Sprites list below it.

4. Drag the Sprites to position them where you want. To delete a Sprite, right-click on it and choose "delete."

5. To choose a backdrop, click the first icon below "New backdrop." This opens the Backdrop Library.

6. Click on the backdrop you want and then click "OK." The backdrop will appear behind your Sprite!

Continued on the next page.

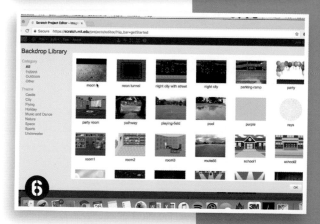

Make Your Sprite Think or Speak

1 Click on your Sprite's icon in your Sprites list. Click "Looks" in the Scripts **panel**.

2 Drag a "say" or "think" Script to the gray panel to the right of the Scripts panel. Then click on the Script. A speech or thought bubble will appear above your Sprite!

3 Change what your Sprite says or thinks by clicking in the Script box and typing new text. Then click on the Script.

4. Add Sprite friends to your scene. Practice making them think or speak!

TIP To delete a Script from the code, just drag it from the gray panel back to the Scripts panel.

Make Your Sprite Move

1. With your Sprite selected, click "Motion" in the Scripts **panel**.

2 Drag a "turn" Script to the gray panel to the right of the Scripts panel. Click on the script to make your Sprite turn.

3 Drag the "move" Script below the turn Script. The two Scripts lock together like puzzle pieces. They create a code. Add more Motion Scripts to your code.

4 You can change how much your Sprite turns and moves by changing the numbers in the Scripts.

5. Click on your Scripts in the gray panel to see your Sprite in action! Scripts that are connected will be performed in a continuous chain.

6. Add more Sprites to your scene. Practice making them move!

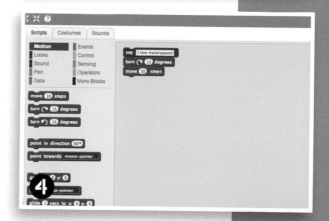

CODE MUSIC

Use Scratch to code your own music!

1. Go to scratch.mit.edu.

2. Click "Try It Out" on the Scratch home page. The program will display a cat character, or Sprite. Delete this Sprite by right-clicking on it and choosing "delete."

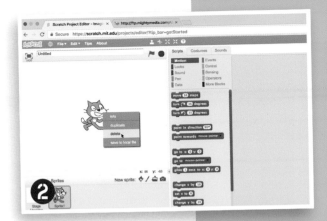

3. Click the first icon next to "New sprite." This opens the Sprite Library.

4. Click "Music" under "Theme" on the sidebar. The library will show only music-related Sprites.

5. Click on the Sprite you want and then click "OK." The new Sprite will appear on the screen and in your Sprites list below it.

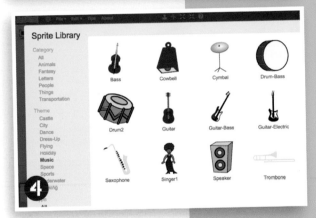

6. To choose a backdrop, click the first icon below "New backdrop." This opens the Backdrop Library. Click on the backdrop you want and then click "OK." The backdrop will appear behind your Sprite!

Continued on the next page.

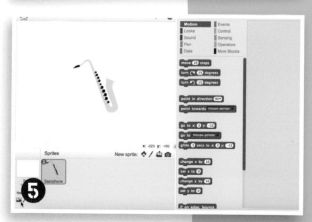

7. Click on your Sprite's icon in your Sprites list. Click "Sound" in the Scripts **panel**.

8 Drag a "play sound" Script to the gray panel to the right of the Scripts panel.

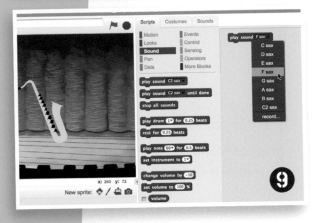

9 Click the arrow on the Script and choose the sound you want from the drop-down menu.

10. Drag another "play sound" Script below the first one. The two Scripts lock together like puzzle pieces. They create a code. Choose a sound for the second Script.

11 Drag the "play note" Script to the bottom of your code. Use the Script's drop-down menu to choose the type of note played. Type the number of beats it should last in the text box.

12 Click "Control" in the Scripts **panel**.

13 Drag the "repeat" Script with a text box to the top of the code. The Script should **automatically** adjust to fit around your existing code.

14. Type the number of times the code should repeat in the "repeat" Script's text box.

15. Click your code to hear your music!

16. Add more music Sprites to your scene. Code Scripts for them to play more music!

TIP You can create many different kinds of Scratch codes. Use the "Tips" menu to learn about the possibilities. Have an adult help you set up a Scratch account. Then you can share your Scratch creations!

BANANA KEY

Turn a banana into a space bar, mouse, or arrow key using a circuit!

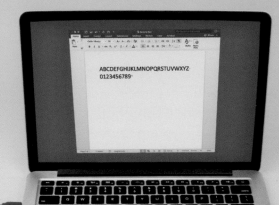

WHAT YOU NEED

Makey Makey Classic kit
(Makey Makey board, USB cable
& alligator clips)

computer with a
word-processing program

banana

ABCDEFGHIJKLMNOPQRSTUVWXYZ
0123456789

1. Plug the small end of the USB cable into the back of the Makey Makey board. Plug the cable's other end into a USB **port** on your computer. If a **pop-up** appears, close it.

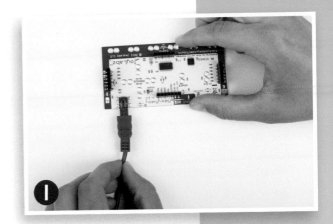

2. Attach one end of an alligator clip to the Makey Makey EARTH bar.

3. Attach one end of another alligator clip to the two SPACE holes. Attach the clip's other end to the stem of a banana.

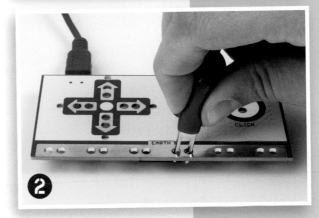

4. Type two lines of text in a word-processing document. It doesn't matter what they say.

5. Hold the loose end of the clip attached to the EARTH bar. Make sure you are touching the metal.

6. Touch the banana with your other hand to close the circuit. Look at your document. Did your banana key insert a space?

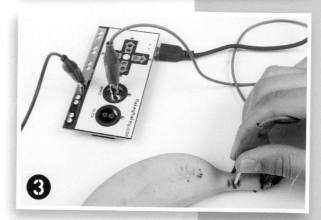

7. Repeat steps 3 through 6, but try using the CLICK or arrow functions on the Makey Makey board.

GAME CONTROLLER

Use Play-Doh to make a working controller!

1. Draw a video game controller shape on the plain cardboard. Cut out the shape. Be sure to cut inside the line so there are no marks on the controller shape.

2. Roll Play-Dough into a small ball. Slightly flatten the ball to make a button for the controller.

3. Repeat step 2 to make three more controller buttons.

4. Press the Play-Doh buttons onto the cardboard controller. Arrange them in a diamond pattern. Make sure the buttons are not touching one another.

Continued on the next page.

TIP If you don't have Play-Doh, you can make your own conductive dough! Look up recipes **online.**

5 Plug the small end of the USB cable into the back of the Makey Makey board.

6. Plug the cable's other end into a USB **port** on your computer. If a **pop-up** appears, close it.

7 Attach one end of an alligator clip to the two holes in the up arrow on the Makey Makey board.

8 Stick the other end of the alligator clip into the corresponding Play-Doh button on your controller.

9 Repeat steps 7 and 8 with the other Makey Makey arrow holes and corresponding Play-Doh buttons.

10 Attach one end of another alligator clip to the Makey Makey EARTH bar.

11. Open a video game that uses arrow keys on your computer. Go to http://makeymakey.com/apps/ to find games you can **download**.

12. Have a friend hold the loose end of the clip attached to the EARTH bar. Make sure he or she is touching the metal.

13. Now you can use your controller to play the game! Each time you touch a Play-Doh button, the circuit closes. This controls the action of the game. Take turns with your friend so you both get to play.

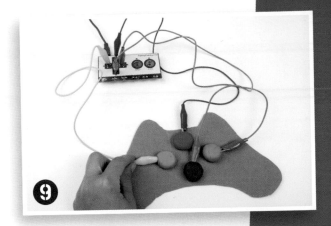

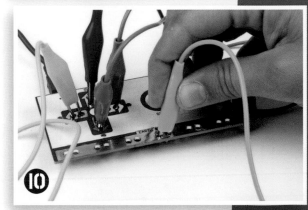

TIP Your game controller must be made with plain cardboard without writing or images on it. These can make the cardboard conductive. The cardboard would then **intercept** the circuit's electricity and the buttons won't work!

25

FLOOR PIANO

Use Makey Makey to create a piano you can play with your feet!

WHAT YOU NEED

large poster boards in two colors

ruler • pencil • scissors

double-sided tape • wire

wire cutter • aluminum tape

Makey Makey Classic kit
(Makey Makey board, USB cable
& alligator clips)

computer with Internet

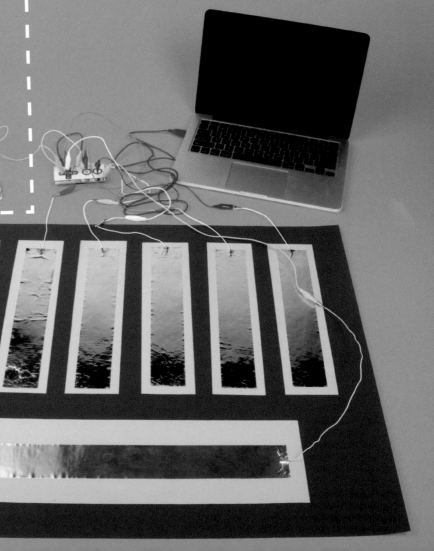

1. Measure the height and width of one of the large poster boards. This board will be the piano.

2. Draw six equal-sized rectangles on the other poster board. Make them each half as long as the height of the piano. Make them each slightly wider than the aluminum tape. Cut them out. These are the piano keys.

3. Cut a slightly larger rectangle out of the same poster board as the keys. This will be the bottom bar.

4. Tape the keys in a row near the top of the piano. Space them evenly so they don't touch one another. Tape the bottom bar below the keys.

5. Cut six pieces of wire, each 3 inches (8 cm) long. These are the short wires.

6. Set the Makey Makey board next to the piano. Cut a long piece of wire. Make sure it will reach from the bottom bar to the Makey Makey board.

Continued on the next page.

27

7 Strip ½ inch (1.25 cm) off both ends of all seven wires.

8 Place a piece of aluminum tape on top of one key. This makes the key conductive! Secure one end of a short wire under the top end of the tape as shown.

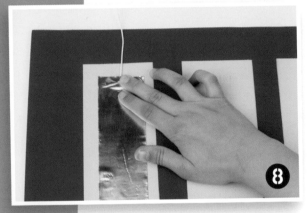

9. Repeat step 8 with the other keys and short wires.

10. Place a piece of aluminum tape on top of the bottom bar. Secure one end of the long wire under one end of the tape.

11 Plug the small end of a USB cable into the back of the Makey Makey board. Plug the other end into the USB **port** of your computer.

12. Go to www.makeymakey.com/piano on your computer. Each piano key corresponds to a key on the Makey Makey board.

13 Connect an alligator clip to the end of the short wire attached to the first piano key.

14. Attach the other end of the alligator clip to the corresponding key on the Makey Makey board.

15. Repeat steps 13 and 14 with the other piano keys.

16 Attach another alligator clip to the EARTH bar. Attach the clip's other end to the end of the long wire.

17. Place one bare foot on the bottom bar. Electricity from the keys and Makey Makey board is now flowing through you!

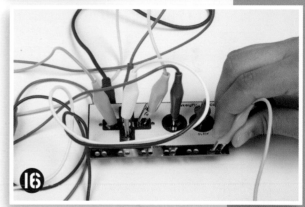

18. Leave your foot on the bottom bar. Touch the keys with your other foot. Each touch closes the circuit. What do you hear?

 TIP To strip a wire, place the wire stripper about ¼ inch (1.25 cm) from the end of the wire. Gently squeeze the handles of the tool and pull the coating off the end of the wire.

MAKERSPACE MAINTENANCE

Being a maker is not just about the finished craft. It's about communicating and **collaborating** with others as you create. The best makers also learn from their creations. They think of ways to improve them next time.

CLEANING UP

When you're done with a project, be sure to tidy up your area. Put away tools and supplies. Make sure they are organized so others can find them easily.

SAFE STORAGE

Sometimes you won't finish a project in one makerspace **session**. That's OK! Just find a safe place to store your project until you can work on it again.

MAKER FOR LIFE!

Maker project possibilities are endless. Get inspired by the materials in your makerspace. Invite new makers to your space. Check out what other makers are creating. Never stop making!

GLOSSARY

automatic – moving or acting by itself.

collaborate – to work with another person or group in order to do something or reach a goal.

download – to transfer data from a computer network to a single computer or device.

intercept – to interrupt something on its way from one place to another.

online – connected to the Internet.

panel – part of a flat surface such as a wall or screen.

permission – when a person in charge says it's okay to do something.

pop-up – a window that suddenly appears on a computer screen.

port – an opening in a device that a wire or cable can be connected to.

saxophone – a woodwind instrument that is made of metal.

session – a period of time used for a specific purpose or activity.

software – the written programs used to operate a computer.

technology – machinery and equipment developed for practical purposes using scientific principles and engineering.

ONLINE RESOURCES

Booklinks
NONFICTION
NETWORK
FREE! ONLINE NONFICTION RESOURCES

To learn more about coding projects, visit **abdobooklinks.com**. These links are routinely monitored and updated to provide the most current information available.

INDEX